We
Shall
Overcome

The Woolworth's Sit-In

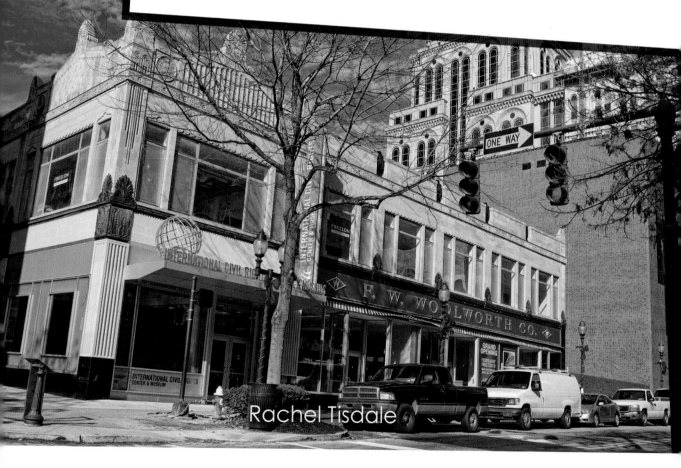

Rachel Tisdale

PowerKiDS
press.

New York

Published in 2014 by The Rosen Publishing Group
29 East 21st Street, New York, NY 10010

Produced for Rosen by Calcium Creative Ltd
Editor for Calcium Creative Ltd: Sarah Eason
US Editor: Joshua Shadowens
Designer: Paul Myerscough

Photo credits: Cover: Corbis: Bettmann. Inside: Corbis: Bettmann 13, Jack
Moebes 16–17; Flickr: Nicolas Henderson 24, Hot Meteor 20; Getty Images:
Howard Sochurek/Time Life Pictures 19; Greensboro Area Convention & Visitors
Bureau: 1, 3, 18, 21, 28; Library of Congress: Painted by F.B. Carpenter; engraved
by A. H. Ritchie 4, Dorothea Lange, FSA/OWI 5, Warren K. Leffler 25; National
Civil Rights Museum: 14; Shutterstock: Action Sports Photography 29, Chippix 6,
Devin_Pavel 9, Maximus256 12; Wikimedia Commons: Dumarest 11, Tony Fischer
15, Jmturner 23, Victor Hugo King 26, Library of Congress, Al Ravenna 7, Ske 10,
White House Press Office/Arnold Newman, 27; www.thehistoryblog.com: 8.

Library of Congress Cataloging-in-Publication Data

Tisdale, Rachel.
  The Woolworth's Sit-In / by Rachel Tisdale.
    pages cm. — (We shall overcome)
  Includes index.
  ISBN 978-1-4777-6065-9 (library) — ISBN 978-1-4777-6066-6 (pbk.) —
  ISBN 978-1-4777-6067-3 (6-pack)
  1. Civil rights movements—Mississippi—History—20th century—Juvenile literature.
  2. African Americans—Civil rights—Mississippi—History—20th century—Juvenile
  literature. 3. African Americans—Segregation—Mississippi—History—20th
  century—Juvenile literature. 4. Mississippi—Race relations—History—20th
  century—Juvenile literature. I. Title.
  E185.93.M6T57 2014
  323.1196'0730762—dc23
                              2013026068

Manufactured in the United States of America

CPSIA Compliance Information: Batch #W14PK5: For Further Information contact Rosen Publishing, New York, New York at 1-800-237-9932

Contents

Slavery and Human Rights

In today's society, all Americans are free to travel and to vote. There are no laws that stop them from getting a good education, and living their lives to the fullest. Life for many Americans, in particular African Americans, was not always this way.

The Slave Trade

From the 1600s to the 1800s, Africans and African Americans were bought and sold as part of the slave trade in America. The slaves had to work hard in the fields, mills, and houses where they lived. By early 1800, most northern states had stopped using slaves. In 1863, President Abraham Lincoln made slavery illegal in the southern states.

President Lincoln (second from the left) ordered that slavery should stop in all southern states.

Not So Free

After 1865, former slaves were able to live free, and by 1870 African American men were able to vote. However, in the southern states, the people in charge introduced literacy tests, poll taxes, and voting systems that stopped many African Americans from voting. The right to vote that had been promised to African Americans was snatched away. Then, other rights were taken away, too.

African Americans were forced to use public places, such as movie theaters, that were kept separate from whites.

Segregation

In the southern states, some white people were afraid of what would happen when slaves became part of their community. They came up with a plan to keep African Americans separate. This became known as segregation.

REX THEATRE FOR COLORED PEOPLE

Separate but Equal

From the 1880s through to the 1960s, southern states enforced Jim Crow laws. These laws segregated African Americans and kept them separate from white people. They restricted contact between whites and other groups, and limited the freedom and rights of African Americans. For example, African American children had to attend different schools from white children, but African American schools were poorly funded.

Jim Crow Laws

Every aspect of public life was controlled by Jim Crow laws. African Americans had to use different entrances to buildings, sit in different places on trains and other public transport, and eat in different restaurants. If they ate in the same restaurant as whites, they had to sit in separate rooms, and each room had to have its own entrance onto the street.

African Americans were banned from sitting with white Americans in their restaurant rooms.

The NAACP

Many African Americans did not agree with segregation. The National Negro Committee came together in 1909, and later changed its name to the National Association for the Advancement of Colored People (NAACP). This organization was formed to defend African Americans against discrimination, and its aim was to secure equal rights.

Railroad Laws

Almost immediately after the Jim Crow laws were introduced, African Americans challenged them. In 1890, a new law was created in Louisiana, which said railroads must provide "equal but separate accommodations for the white, and colored, races." On June 7, 1892, African American Homer Plessy took a seat reserved for whites on a railroad car. He was arrested for refusing to move. The case went to the US Supreme Court. On May 18, 1896, the Court ruled that "separate" facilities for African Americans and white Americans was lawful, as long as the facilities were "equal."

Both African American and white NAACP members campaigned for an end to segregation in the South.

Civil Rights Organizations

From the 1940s onward, the movement for civil rights gathered pace and several organizations were set up to promote racial equality and end segregation. These organizations often worked together to plan joint peaceful protests, such as boycotts and sit-ins. In a sit-in, people protest by sitting down in a place and refusing to move.

Nonviolence

The Congress of Racial Equality (CORE) was formed in 1942, in Chicago. It was created by a group of African American and white students, who organized sit-ins in public places to protest against segregation. Once they had managed to end segregation in public facilities in the North, CORE decided to focus its attention on the South.

Martin Luther King Jr. is remembered today as the most prominent leader of the American Civil Rights Movement.

Saving America

In 1957, shortly after the success of the Montgomery Bus Boycott, the key leaders of the protest met and formed the Southern Christian Leadership Conference (SCLC). Martin Luther King Jr., who was a prominent figure in the civil rights movement, was to be the president of the organization. The group helped to organize and aid the action of local protest groups in the South, with the aim of "redeeming 'the Soul of America' through nonviolent resistance."

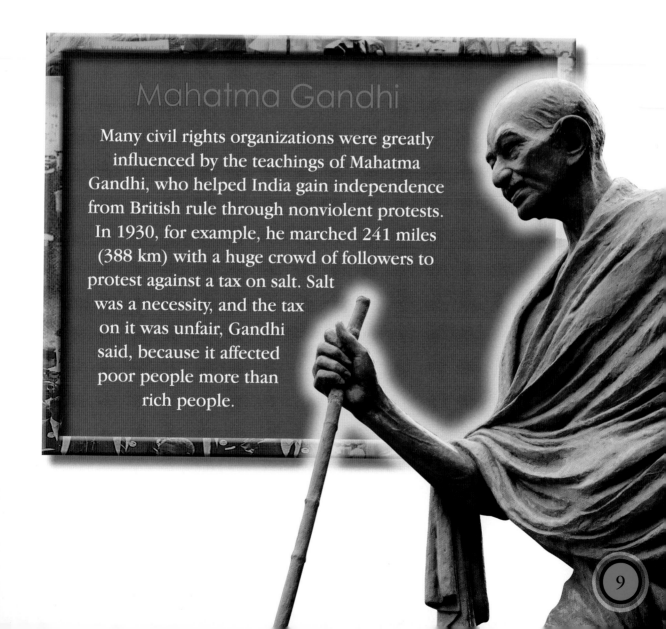

Mahatma Gandhi

Many civil rights organizations were greatly influenced by the teachings of Mahatma Gandhi, who helped India gain independence from British rule through nonviolent protests. In 1930, for example, he marched 241 miles (388 km) with a huge crowd of followers to protest against a tax on salt. Salt was a necessity, and the tax on it was unfair, Gandhi said, because it affected poor people more than rich people.

Challenging the Law

During the 1950s, the main aim of civil rights organizations was to challenge the segregation laws in court. In 1896, the US Supreme Court had said that separate facilities for African Americans and white Americans was lawful, provided they were equal. Conditions for African Americans, however, were seldom equal to those for whites. In 1954, a new case was put before the Court.

A New Law

The case was called *Brown v. Board of Education*. It was brought on behalf of several African American children who wanted to attend white schools to get a better education.

African American parents and their children took to the streets to protest against inequality in American schools.

In the 1950s, schools for white children had better books, tables, chairs, and school buildings than schools for African American children. The Court decided that denying African American children access to white schools was against the law. This was a victory for civil rights campaigners, and soon more changes began to happen.

The Montgomery Bus Boycott

Greensboro Gillespie Park Elementary School

After the *Brown v. Board of Education* decision, Greensboro, North Carolina, became the first city in the South to publicly announce that it would follow the decision and start desegregating its schools. In 1957, five African American children entered Gillespie Park Elementary School.

In 1955, in Montgomery, Alabama, Rosa Parks refused to give up her seat to a white passenger when traveling on a public transport bus. She was soon arrested and jailed. With help from supporters, Rosa inspired a boycott in Montgomery in which hundreds of African Americans chose not to ride the city's buses. Over a year later, a court ruling forced the bus companies to finally desegregate the buses, and African Americans could sit where they liked.

Rosa Parks' arrest inspired a boycott in which thousands of African Americans refused to ride the city's segregated buses.

The Sit-In Begins

On February 1, 1960, four African American students in their freshman year at college in Greensboro, North Carolina, decided to take peaceful direct action rather than challenge the segregation laws in court. They planned to protest against segregation in restaurants by staging a sit-in. They chose Woolworth's department store, because they thought it was unfair that they could shop in the store, but not eat at its lunch counter.

Greensboro, North Carolina, was the site of the first sit-in protest against segregation in public places.

Washington, D.C.

Greensboro

NORTH CAROLINA

The Heroic Four

Just before 4.30 p.m., Franklin McCain, Joseph McNeil, David Richmond, and Ezell Blair Jr. stepped into their local Woolworth's department store and bought some items. They then sat down at the lunch counter, which was for white customers only. The students asked for service, but were refused and told to leave. They politely remained in their seats until the lunch counter was forced to close early. They returned to the college as heroes.

On February 2, more African American students joined the sit-in protest.

Gathering Support

The next day, the men returned to Woolworth's lunch counter, along with 15 other supporters. Again, they ordered and were refused service, but sat at the counter peacefully. On day three, they had 85 supporters. On day four, African American students were joined by white female students from the North Carolina's Women's College. By the end of the week, more than 400 supporters had joined the cause.

"I had a feeling of liberation, restored manhood. I had a natural high. And I truly felt almost invincible. Mind you, [I was] just sitting on a dumb stool and not having asked for service yet."
Franklin McCain.

Violence and Humiliation

The sit-in caused so much disruption at the Woolworth's store that it was forced to close its restaurant on February 10, just one week after the sit-in had started. The students were not deterred, however, and they continued sit-ins at other lunch counters across the city.

Humiliation

It was not always easy for the students sitting at the lunch counters. The students had agreed to follow certain rules and always had to act peacefully. However, they were often faced with verbal and physical abuse. The students were shouted at and pushed. They had ketchup, hot drinks, and itching powder poured on them.

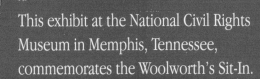

This exhibit at the National Civil Rights Museum in Memphis, Tennessee, commemorates the Woolworth's Sit-In.

All the time, the students had to remain calm and continue sitting, until another student took their place.

Sit-In Rules

The rules sit-in students followed were:
- Be friendly on the counter.
- Sit straight and face the counter.
- Do not strike, or curse back, if attacked.
- Do not laugh out loud.
- Do not hold conversations.
- Do not block entrances.

Ella Baker

Ella Baker played a major role in helping student protesters and activists. She was born in Norfolk, Virginia, on December 13, 1903. She moved to New York in 1927, where she worked for the NAACP. In 1957, Ella moved to Atlanta to organize the SCLC's campaign to enforce voting rights for African American citizens. Inspired by the success of the Woolworth's Sit-In, she contacted students on other campuses to tell them what was happening in Greensboro.

Ella Baker and three other great civil rights campaigners are remembered on this mural in Philadelphia, Pennsylvania.

"WE WHO BELIEVE IN FREEDOM CANNOT REST."
ELLA BAKER AND THE BIRTH OF S.N.C.C.

MALCOLM SHABAZZ   ELLA BAKER   MARTIN LUTHER KING   FREDERICK DOUGLASS

FOUR AMERICAN PATRIOTS WHO DEDICATED THEIR LIVES TO CIVIL RIGHTS AND A BETTER AMERICA

The Sit-Ins Spread

News of the Woolworth's Sit-Ins spread to students on other campuses. Inspired by the Greensboro students, students in many other cities began to take part in sit-ins. Protests took place in cities across North Carolina, including Winston-Salem, Durham, Raleigh, Charlotte, Fayetteville, High Point, Elizabeth City, and Concord. The sit-ins mostly took place at Woolworth's stores, but also at S. H. Kress stores.

In the News

The sit-ins were widely covered in the news. After hearing about the sit-ins on television and in newspaper reports, people started to take notice. More and more students across the South copied the Greensboro example of direct, peaceful action. By February 7, 54 sit-ins were in place throughout the South, in nine separate states.

"... an electrifying movement of Negro students shattered the placid surface of campuses and communities across the South."
Martin Luther King Jr., describing the sit-ins.

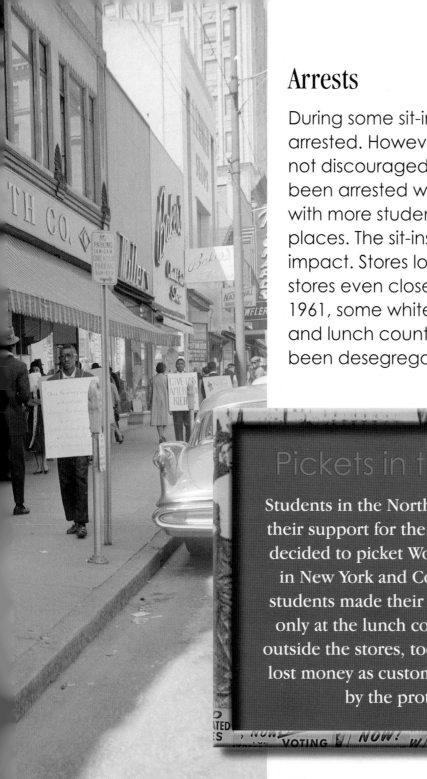

Arrests

During some sit-ins, students were arrested. However, the students were not discouraged, and those who had been arrested were soon replaced with more students, who took their places. The sit-ins were making an impact. Stores lost money and some stores even closed. By September 1961, some white-owned restaurants and lunch counters in Atlanta had been desegregated.

Pickets in the North

Students in the North wanted to show their support for the sit-ins, too. They decided to picket Woolworth's stores in New York and Connecticut. The students made their voices heard not only at the lunch counters, but also outside the stores, too. The businesses lost money as customers were put off by the protesters.

African Americans picketed Woolworth stores to demand treatment equal to that of white Americans.

Nashville, Tennessee

Shortly after the Greensboro Sit-In, students from Nashville, Tennessee, began to protest against segregation in their community, too. The students followed the tactics used at Greensboro. They sat quietly at lunch counters across the city. The Greensboro protesters encountered violence, but in Nashville the response was more extreme.

Gassing

In one of the worst incidents, the manager of one Nashville restaurant tried to stop the sit-in by turning on a fumigating machine, which filled the restaurant with insecticide gas. Students were trapped inside the restaurant, where it was almost impossible to breathe.

To Jail

So many students in Nashville were arrested that the jail overflowed with students in horribly crowded cells.

This is the lunch counter and chairs of the Woolworth's store where the original sit-in took place.

18

Students prepared for sit-ins by subjecting each other to the treatment they would receive from white Americans against desegregation.

In total, over 150 students were arrested during the sit-ins in the city.

Bombing

Z. Alexander Looby was an African American lawyer and councillor who lived in Nashville and supported the sit-ins. Looby defended the students who had been arrested, but in doing so, he put himself in grave danger. On April 19, 1960, his house was bombed while he and his wife were sleeping. Luckily, neither Looby nor his wife were injured.

Smart Appearance

As well as behaving politely and quietly, the students attending the sit-in protests always dressed smartly, in their best clothes. It was important to look well dressed and act in an appropriate manner. The students' appearance worked in their favor. On news reports and in photographs, they looked far smarter than the white Americans who came to heckle them. The protesters filled their time at the lunch counters by studying and reading.

News of the bombing at Z. Alexander Looby's home spread. He was well respected in the city by both African Americans and many white people. Later that day, more than 2,500 protesters gathered to march silently to the city hall to speak with the mayor of Nashville, Ben West.

Meeting the Mayor

Diane Nash was one of the people who marched to the city hall and met with the mayor. She was a member of the Nashville Student Movement and had helped to organize many of the sit-in protests across the city. The marchers demanded that the lunch counters in the city be desegregated. In this meeting, Ben West said that segregation and discrimination were "wrong and immoral." The mayor put together an agreement between civil rights leaders and businesses in the city to desegregate lunch counters.

Outraged protesters marched to the city hall in Nashville (above) to demand a move toward full desegregation from the city's mayor.

Success in Nashville

Nashville became the first major city in the South to begin desegregating its public facilities. On May 10, 1960, six stores in Nashville desegregated their lunch counters. This was a victory for civil rights in Nashville, but in Greensboro, and other parts of the country, the protests continued.

Fisk University

On April 21, Martin Luther King Jr. visited Nashville and addressed a mass meeting at Fisk University. He praised the Nashville sit-in movement as "the best organized and the most disciplined in the Southland." He told the audience to continue with the sit-in demonstrations. He proclaimed "We will say, do what you will to us, but we will wear you down by our capacity to suffer."

The first four students who took part in the Woolworth's Sit-In are remembered in this statue in Greensboro.

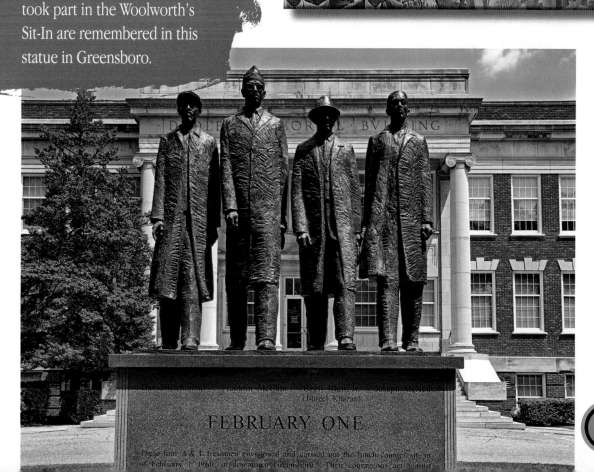

FEBRUARY ONE

The Protests Spread

Peaceful sit-ins spread, with more than 70,000 people taking part in sit-ins across the United States. The sit-ins even spread to states farther north, such as Illinois and Ohio, and the western state of Nevada. People could see that silent, peaceful protests worked, because they showed how unfair American society was at the time. White Americans against desegregation, however, did not give up.

More Violence

In Jackson, Mississippi, the violence against the sit-in protesters was taken to another level. At a sit-in at the Woolworth's store, protesters were beaten, burned, and attacked with broken glass.

John Salter (foreground) was sprayed with food and beaten on the back and head at the sit-in in Jackson.

In an effort to put off students, some stores even removed the stools from lunch counters to avoid student sit-ins.

Other Public Places

Sit-ins were not used only to protest about segregation at food counters. People used them to protest about segregated swimming pools, libraries, transport facilities, museums, art galleries, parks, and beaches.

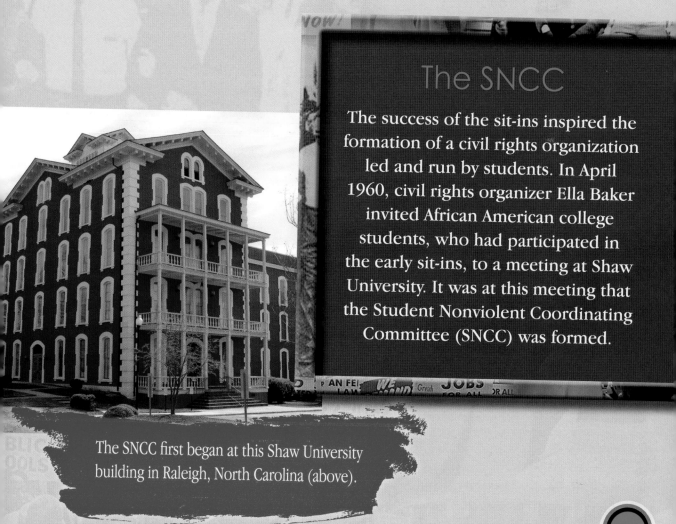

The SNCC

The success of the sit-ins inspired the formation of a civil rights organization led and run by students. In April 1960, civil rights organizer Ella Baker invited African American college students, who had participated in the early sit-ins, to a meeting at Shaw University. It was at this meeting that the Student Nonviolent Coordinating Committee (SNCC) was formed.

The SNCC first began at this Shaw University building in Raleigh, North Carolina (above).

Victory in Sight

Five months after the four students sat down at the lunch counter in Greensboro, the Woolworth's store eventually agreed to desegregate its food counter. Four of its African American employees were the first people to be served. Due to the closure of the lunch counter and disruption from the sit-ins, the company had lost over $200,000 dollars of business.

The Freedom Rides

Inspired by the achievements of the student sit-ins, CORE decided to test segregation on public buses and in bus stations in the southern states. In 1961, Freedom Riders refused to sit in racially segregated areas of the buses.

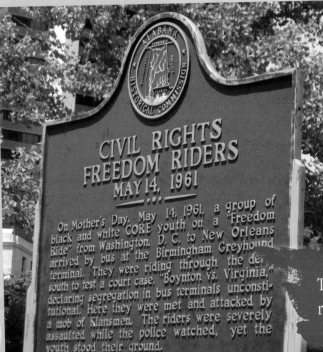

CIVIL RIGHTS
FREEDOM RIDERS
MAY 14, 1961

On Mother's Day, May 14, 1961, a group of black and white CORE youth on a "Freedom Ride" from Washington, D.C. to New Orleans arrived by bus at the Birmingham Greyhound terminal. They were riding through the deep south to test a court case, "Boynton vs. Virginia," declaring segregation in bus terminals unconstitutional. Here they were met and attacked by a mob of Klansmen. The riders were severely assaulted while the police watched, yet the youth stood their ground.

"When I did see the young people, first the sit-ins and the courage that they had to have, and then ... [on] the bus in Anniston, ... I thought I just had to do something, and simply volunteered and proceeded."
Albert Gordon, Freedom Rider.

This marker in Birmingham, Alabama, remembers the Freedom Riders.

African American riders sat in "whites only" waiting rooms at the bus stations, too. The Freedom Riders encountered bombings, beatings, and jail before the government acted to enforce desegregation in the southern states.

Around 250,000 people took part in the March on Washington for Jobs and Freedom on August 28, 1963.

March on Washington

After the success of the Freedom Rides and other protests across the country, civil rights organizations planned a march to Washington, D.C. It was known as the March on Washington for Jobs and Freedom. Protesters demanded a civil rights bill that would ensure better education, housing, and voting rights for African Americans.

Legalizing Equality

The protests of the civil rights movement showed the government of the United States that people wanted changes in the law, and would not give up until they were achieved. President John. F. Kennedy began to draw up a civil rights bill that would end segregation across the United States.

Death and Hope

However, in 1963, while the details of the bill were being processed, the president was assassinated in Dallas, Texas. His successor, President Lyndon B. Johnson, made

President Kennedy was assassinated as he rode through Dallas in an open-top car.

"This law covers many pages, but the heart of the Act is plain. Wherever, by clear and objective standards, States and counties are using regulations, or laws, or tests to deny the right to vote, then they will be struck down."
President Lyndon B. Johnson (left).

it his mission to push through the civil rights bill as a tribute to the late President Kennedy. In July of the following year, the Civil Rights Act was signed, making all Americans equal by law. African Americans could now hope to achieve good jobs, education, and not have to face discrimination in public places.

Voting Rights

Injustice still remained, however. Although everyone had the right to vote, 98 percent of African Americans in Selma, Alabama, were prevented from voting because they could not first pass a literacy test. In 1965, there were several peaceful marches through Selma to demand the right of African Americans to vote. Many of the marchers faced violence and imprisonment. Finally, on August 6, 1965, the Voting Rights Act was signed and African Americans were allowed to vote without first having to pass a literacy test.

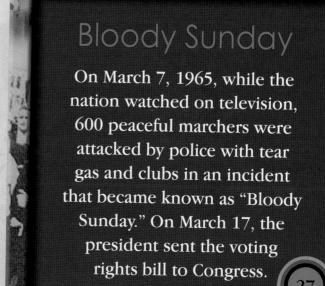

Bloody Sunday

On March 7, 1965, while the nation watched on television, 600 peaceful marchers were attacked by police with tear gas and clubs in an incident that became known as "Bloody Sunday." On March 17, the president sent the voting rights bill to Congress.

A Lasting Legacy

The Greensboro Four and the Woolworth's Sit-In gave the civil rights movement new energy. Instead of arguing their cause in court, these young people took peaceful direct action to focus the attention of the media and the public on the injustice of Jim Crow laws. Their protest continued until their demands were finally accepted.

Civil Rights Museum

The Woolworth's building in Greensboro, where the sit-ins started, is now home to the International Civil Rights Center and Museum. Visitors can experience the struggle of the civil rights movement through photographs, videos, and artifacts in the museum's "The Battlegrounds" exhibit.

Each year, thousands of people visit the International Civil Rights Center and Museum, the site of the original Woolworth's Sit-In.

"Hope is the bedrock of this nation. The belief that our destiny will not be written for us, but by us, by all those men and women who are not content to settle for the world as it is, who have the courage to remake the world as it should be."
President Barack Obama.

First African American President

In 2008, Barack Obama (above) became the first African American to be elected as President of the United States. Without the brave men and women who took part in the peaceful sit-ins, this may not have been possible.

Motivation for Change

The Greensboro Four helped to bring about a monumental change in the history of the United States. The sit-ins at Greensboro motivated hundreds of citizens across the country to campaign for civil rights. In doing so, they helped to change the laws that discriminated against African Americans forever.

Glossary

abuse (uh-BYOOS) To hurt someone or something verbally or physically.

activist (AK-tih-vist) Someone who stands up for what they believe in.

boycott (BOY-kot) To refuse to use.

campaign (kam-PAYN) A series of planned actions to reach a particular goal.

civil rights (SIH-vul RYTS) The rights given by a government to all its citizens.

community (kuh-MYOO-nih-tee) A group of people who live close together or have shared interests.

Congress (KON-gres) The branch of the US government that makes laws.

democracy (dih-MAH-kruh-see) A government in which people have power through the representatives they elect.

desegregated (dee-SEH-gruh-gayt-ed) To stop the use of separate schools and facilities for people of different races.

discrimination (dis-krih-muh-NAY-shun) Treating some people differently from others.

elected (ee-LEK-tid) When a person is voted for by the people of a country to serve in that country's government.

freshman (FRESH-mun) A student in the first year of high school, college, or university.

fumigating (FYOO-muh-gay-ting) The release of chemical fumes.

immoral (ih-MOR-ul) Bad.

insecticide (in-SEK-tih-syd) A poison used to kill insects.

picket (PIH-ket) A group of people who stand in front of a building or business to protest or demand something.

poll tax (POHL TAKS) A tax a person has to pay for the right to vote.

segregation (seh-gruh-GAY-shun) A system to keep white Americans and African Americans apart.

sit-in (SIT-in) A form of protest where people sit down and refuse to move.

Supreme Court (suh-PREEM KORT) The highest court in the United States.

trespassing (TRES-pas-sing) Entering somewhere without permission.

tribute (TRIH-byoot) Something given, done, or said to express thanks or respect.

verbal (VER-bul) Spoken words.

voting rights (VOH-ting RYTS) The right to vote.

Further Reading

Cregan, Elizabeth R. *Independence and Equality*. World Black History. Mankato, MN: Capstone Press, 2011.

Foy, Debbie. *Civil-Rights Activists*. Black History Makers. New York: PowerKids Press, 2012.

Jeffrey, Gary. *Martin Luther King Jr. and the March on Washington*. A Graphic History of the Civil Rights Movement. New York: Gareth Stevens Learning Library, 2012.

Websites

Due to the changing nature of Internet links, PowerKids Press has developed an online list of websites related to the subject of this book. This site is updated regularly. Please use this link to access the list:
www.powerkidslinks.com/wso/sitin/

Index

DATE DUE